WORKBOOK

For

WORTHY

By

Jamie Kern Lima

**Exercises & Prompts For Processing,
Practicing and Implementing the Lesson**

Table of Content

WORTHY STARTS HERE

You Become What You Believe You're Worthy of

The introduction of "Worthy" by Jamie Kern Lima delves deep into the theme of self-worth and its profound impact on our lives. It begins by recounting relatable scenarios from childhood to adulthood where self-doubt and feelings of unworthiness influence our actions and decisions. Lima emphasizes how self-doubt dims our inner light, leading us to play it safe, hold back, and hide our true selves. She candidly shares her personal journey, including moments of self-sabotage and missed opportunities rooted in feelings of unworthiness.

The author highlights the pivotal role of self-belief in achieving our goals and dreams.

Lima shares her own experience of meeting Oprah Winfrey and realizing that her lack of belief in her own worthiness had held her back from seizing opportunities. She stresses that regardless of our aspirations or efforts, if we don't fundamentally believe we are worthy of success, love, and fulfillment, we will struggle to attain them.

Throughout the introduction, Lima encourages readers to confront their own self-doubt and embrace their inherent worthiness. She underscores the transformative power of believing in oneself, asserting that it is the key to unlocking one's full potential and living a fulfilling life. The author sets the stage for a journey of self-discovery and empowerment, inviting readers to explore their relationship with self-worth and embrace the truth that they are worthy of love and success.

PART ONE
SEEING

Self-Confidence, Self-Worth, and Self-Revelations

CHAPTER ONE

The One Thing That Transforms Everything

Chapter 1 of the book delves into the pivotal concept of self-worth and its transformative power in our lives. It opens with a poignant quote about perseverance and introduces the idea of seeking external achievements or milestones in hopes of finding fulfillment. The author shares personal experiences and insights, highlighting a common belief that achieving certain goals will lead to feelings of worthiness and happiness. However, through years of growth and interacting with successful individuals, the author realizes that the pursuit of external validation alone doesn't address the deeper sense of unworthiness many people experience.

This chapter distinguishes between self-worth and self-confidence, emphasizing that while self-confidence relates to one's abilities and accomplishments, self-worth is an inherent belief in one's value and enoughness. Despite the societal emphasis on building self-confidence, the author argues that true fulfillment comes from nurturing self-worth, which remains stable regardless of external circumstances. Self-worth serves as the foundation for confidence, resilience, and authentic living, enabling individuals to pursue their goals without being hindered by feelings of inadequacy or fear of failure.

This chapter discusses the pitfalls of relying solely on self-confidence without addressing underlying issues of self-worth. Even with external success, individuals may still feel unfulfilled if they lack a deep sense of worthiness. The author challenges conventional solutions focused on external validation and encourages readers to embark on a journey of cultivating self-worth, recognizing its profound impact on every aspect of life. The author emphasizes the importance of self-worth in achieving true fulfillment and happiness. She discusses how many people chase external achievements, such as wealth or success, in the hopes of feeling worthy and loved. However, true fulfillment comes from recognizing one's innate value and worthiness, separate from external accomplishments. The author also distinguishes between self-confidence and self-worth, highlighting that while self-confidence is important, it must be built upon a foundation of self-worth to lead to lasting fulfillment. It concludes by emphasizing the need to prioritize building self-worth as a key to experiencing deep happiness and resilience in life.

KEYTAKEAWAYS FROM CHAPTER ONE

Self-Worth vs. Self-Confidence:
Understand the difference between self-worth and self-confidence. While self-confidence relates to abilities and accomplishments, self-worth is an inherent belief in one's value and enoughness.

External Validation vs. Intrinsic Worth:
Recognize the pitfalls of seeking external validation for feelings of worthiness and happiness. True fulfillment comes from recognizing one's innate value separate from external achievements.

Foundation of Self-Worth:
Emphasize the importance of cultivating self-worth as the foundation for confidence, resilience, and authentic living. Without a strong sense of self-worth, external success may not lead to lasting fulfillment.

SELF DEVELOPMENTAL WORKBOOK

PROMPTS

Take some time to reflect on your beliefs about your inherent value and enoughness. Are your feelings of worthiness tied to external achievements or do you recognize your intrinsic worth

While i "know" I am intrinsicly worthy, I also know I am blocked + have work to do because I do self-sabotage. My income + business is not producing the results I want.

Identify any limiting beliefs you hold about yourself that may be hindering your sense of self-worth (e.g., "I'm not good enough", "I need to achieve more to be worthy"). How do these beliefs impact your actions and decisions?

13

I AM worthy to be prosperous
living in my purpose, being a millionaire
owning a home, getting out of debt
Not over spending. I deeply struggle
with perfection + body image. I have
come a LONG way - I am proud of that.
i know there is more enough.

Brainstorm ways you can cultivate self-worth in your
daily life. This could include practicing self-compassion,
affirmations, or engaging in activities that bring you joy
and fulfillment independent of external validation.

Working through this book. Taking
care of my body because it feels good
Eat healthy, Drink water. PRAY

Read the Bible

Go back to Church

Set an intention to prioritize building self-worth over
seeking external validation in the coming weeks. How
will you incorporate this intention into your daily routine
and decision-making process?

I will recognize when I am
seeking external validation
+ remind myself that I am
worthy no matter what.

Write about a time when you achieved a significant external milestone (e.g., landing a job, reaching a financial goal). How did you feel upon achieving it? Did it bring lasting fulfillment or a temporary sense of accomplishment?

Last year, I made 100K (very close to it). I was very proud of myself + it brough a very big lesson of how much money I spend to light.

Every dollar in went right back out. I want to really uncover my block with worthiness around money + my business + have no fear of being seen.

Chapter Two

Change Your Relationship With Rejection, Change Your Life

This chapter explores the transformative power of changing our relationship with rejection and failure. The author begins by sharing personal experiences of facing rejection and how it almost prevented her from pursuing various endeavors in her life. She discusses how fear of rejection and failure often holds people back from taking chances and pursuing their dreams. The author emphasizes that rejection and failure are not inherently negative but rather carry the meaning we assign to them. By changing the meaning we attach to rejection and failure, we can shift our emotional responses and life experiences.

The author illustrates this concept through anecdotes, including her own experience with rosacea and the moment she decided to redefine its meaning. She shares how embracing her perceived imperfections empowered her and inspired others. Additionally, the author recounts her journey of building her company, IT Cosmetics, and defying conventional advice by showcasing real women with skin challenges in her marketing campaigns. Despite facing numerous rejections, she

remained steadfast in her belief and ultimately achieved success.

This chapter urges readers with practical steps for changing one's relationship with rejection, emphasizing the importance of self-awareness and persistence in this process. The author acknowledges that it takes time and effort to unlearn old patterns and create new ones but believes that it is essential for personal growth and empowerment. Overall, the chapter encourages readers to embrace rejection as an opportunity for growth and to fearlessly pursue their aspirations. The excerpt outlines a four-step process called "The Four Rs to Transcending Rejection," which aims to empower individuals to redefine their relationship with rejection and failure.

1. Reveal: The first step involves identifying one's default definitions of rejection and failure and recognizing how these definitions shape one's perception and response to rejection. It highlights the importance of acknowledging and challenging these default beliefs to avoid being stuck in fear and self-doubt.

2. Redefine: This step encourages individuals to create new, empowering definitions of rejection and failure that alleviate the fear associated with them. By assigning positive meanings to these experiences, individuals can shift their mindset and approach rejection with confidence.

3. Revisit and Reframe: Here, individuals are prompted to reflect on past rejections and failures, assigning new meanings to these experiences that empower them rather than hold them back. By reframing past setbacks as opportunities for growth and learning, individuals can find peace and move forward.

4. Revel: The final step involves embracing rejection as part of the journey towards success and personal growth. By adopting a mindset of resilience and courage, individuals can fear rejection less and pursue their goals with confidence and determination.

Overall, the process emphasizes the importance of changing one's perspective on rejection and failure to overcome fear and self-doubt, ultimately leading to personal growth and success

KEYTAKEAWAYS FROM CHAPTER TWO

Transformative Power of Changing Perspectives:
Rejection and failure are not inherently negative; they carry the meaning we assign to them. By changing our perspective, we can shift our emotional responses and life experiences.

Embracing Imperfections:
The author's experience with rosacea illustrates the empowerment that comes from embracing perceived imperfections and redefining their meaning.

Persistence in the Face of Rejection:
Despite facing numerous rejections in her journey to build IT Cosmetics, the author remained steadfast in her belief and ultimately achieved success.

The Four Rs to Transcending Rejection:

The chapter outlines a four-step process - Reveal, Redefine, Revisit and Reframe, and Revel - aimed at empowering individuals to redefine their relationship with rejection and failure.

SELF DEVELOPMENTAL WORKBOOK
PROMPTS

Reflect on your default definitions of rejection and
failure. How do these definitions shape your perception
and response to rejection? Write down any patterns or
recurring thoughts.

Rejection + Failure - I have a pretty

healthy grasp of failure but rejection

hurts. I'm not good enough

+ not inherintly lovable Even though

I know I am worthy, there is a

deep block there.

Take some time to create new, empowering definitions of rejection and failure for yourself. How can you assign positive meanings to these experiences to shift your mindset and approach rejection with confidence?

I love the thought that God had hid
my value to some because they
are not meant for my journey.
Man's rejection really is God's
protection - in His timing, the
right people assigned to my destiny
will appear. ♥

Think about past rejections and failures in your life. How can you reframe these experiences to see them as opportunities for growth and learning? Write down new meanings you can assign to these setbacks that empower you rather than hold you back.

God has something better

God is working behind the scenes,

Consider how adopting a mindset of resilience and courage can help you fear rejection less and pursue your goals with confidence and determination. How can you cultivate resilience in the face of rejection? List specific actions you can take to strengthen your resilience.

Staying in the Word

Share your life - live in the light &

use social for good

PRAY

Reflect on how you can apply the four-step process -
Reveal, Redefine, Revisit and Reframe, and Revel - in
your own life. Write down concrete steps you can take to
implement each of these steps and begin transforming
your relationship with rejection and failure.

Catch yourself + remember God's

truth .

CHAPTER THREE

You're Not Crazy, You're Just First.

Chapter Three delves into the concept of being "first" in embracing authenticity and individuality. The author shares anecdotes of individuals who were considered unconventional in their ideas, such as the creator of the Pet Rock and the Wright brothers, highlighting the doubt and ridicule they faced before achieving success. Drawing from personal experiences of being labeled "crazy" for her ambitious ideas and different perspectives, the author reflects on the journey of self-discovery and acceptance. She emphasizes the importance of authenticity and self-awareness in challenging societal norms and pursuing one's unique path. This chapter encourages readers to reframe their perception of themselves as "first" rather than "crazy," embracing their individuality and pursuing their dreams with courage. It also discusses the impact of authenticity on forming genuine connections and finding fulfillment in life. Through practical insights and reflections, the author inspires readers to embrace their uniqueness and live authentically, knowing that they are the only "first" version of themselves in the world.

KEYTAKEAWAYS FROM CHAPTER THREE

Embrace authenticity:

Chapter three explores the concept of being "first" in embracing authenticity and individuality.

Overcoming doubt:

The author shares anecdotes of individuals who faced doubt and ridicule for their unconventional ideas before achieving success.

Self-discovery journey:

Drawing from personal experiences, the author reflects on the journey of self-discovery and acceptance.

Reframe perceptions:

Readers are encouraged to reframe their perception of themselves as "first" rather than "crazy," embracing their uniqueness.

Impact of authenticity:

The chapter discusses the impact of authenticity on forming genuine connections and finding fulfillment in life.

SELF DEVELOPMENTAL WORKBOOK

PROMPTS

Reflect on a time when you felt pressured to conform to societal norms or hide your true self. How did this impact your sense of identity and fulfillment?

What comes to mind most is with "Christianity." I remember not wanting to post about Halloween for fear of judgment. It's so silly but just being judged by Christians holds me back - and also not eating meat.

Consider the moments in your life when you were called names like "crazy" or "different." How did these labels shape your self-perception? How can you reframe these perceptions to see yourself as "first"?

I kind of like being called crazy,
but I don't like being judged for being
"perfect." That's when I play small +
dim my light. "Who does she think
she is" energy.

Explore the importance of authenticity in forming
genuine connections with others. Have you ever
experienced a deep connection with someone who
showed up authentically? How did it impact your
relationship?

I really value authenticity
+ admire that when I see it
unapologetically in others.

Imagine a world where everyone embraced their uniqueness and lived authentically. How would society benefit from this collective shift towards embracing individuality?

we would not all try to conform

we would be more inclusive

& open-minded

Write a letter to your younger self, offering words of encouragement and wisdom about embracing authenticity and being "first" in your own journey. What advice would you give yourself?

Live in the light. You were born to be a leader + influence others to live in vision, believe in God, and transform their lives.

CHAPTER FOUR

You Have Greatness Inside You

Chapter 4 delves deep into the theme of recognizing and unlocking the greatness within ourselves, regardless of our past experiences or circumstances. The chapter begins by emphasizing that everyone has greatness inside them, but believing in it and embracing it is crucial. Often, doubts about our own worthiness and capabilities hold us back from realizing our potential. The author shares personal anecdotes, including her journey of enduring setbacks in business and her ongoing struggle to feel worthy. Despite facing challenges and making mistakes, she emphasizes that our past doesn't define us and it's never too late to start anew.

The author shares intimate details about her upbringing, including her relationship with her parents, particularly her alcoholic father. Despite the difficulties she faced, she excelled in school but yearned for validation and attention. As a teenager, she fell in with a troubled crowd and got involved in risky behavior, which ultimately led to her arrest. The experience was a wake-up call, prompting her to reflect on her choices and the direction of her life.Although she was released with a hefty community service sentence, the author admits that it didn't feel like a fresh start. She continued to struggle, skipping school and seeking validation from her peers. Despite these challenges, she found success in her job at a health club, where her natural sales skills propelled her into a managerial role at a young age. However, she also found herself drawn to forbidden relationships, highlighting the allure of the unknown.

Chapter four explores the journey of self-discovery and overcoming past mistakes to embrace one's own greatness, demonstrating that resilience and determination can lead to personal growth and fulfillment. The author reflects on her relationship with Brad, where they kept their romance secret due to their working relationship. However, the author's feelings grew stronger, as watching Brad date multiple women became painful. Despite asking Brad to be exclusive, he refused, leading the author to feel torn between breaking up and abandoning the relationship or staying and abandoning herself. Ultimately, she chose to abandon herself, feeling consumed by pain when apart from Brad.

The author reflects on her growing dissatisfaction despite her financial success and dreams of going to college. Despite her father's opposition to college, she decides to enroll in a summer semester using her savings from the job at the health club. Eventually, she transitioned to working part-time at a grocery store and Denny's while waitressing at a strip club in a nearby city. While working at the strip club, the author forms bonds with the waitresses and dancers, gaining insight into their struggles and aspirations. She realizes that these women, often judged by society, are resilient and have similar hopes and dreams as anyone else.

The author recounts a brief romance with a customer from the strip club, which ends abruptly due to their realization of incompatibility and feeling unsafe. These experiences prompt the author to reflect her search for love and worthiness outside, leading her to explore faith and personal development through attending church and a Tony Robbins seminar.

These moments of grace and personal growth lead the author to make significant life changes, including leaving the strip club, pursuing higher education, and ultimately founding a successful business. Despite setbacks and challenges, the author emphasizes the importance of trusting oneself and embracing grace in one's life journey. The author also reflects on her journey toward self-worth and the realization that external validation does not equate to true fulfillment. The author highlights the transformative power of service and the belief that everyone has the potential for greatness through acts of kindness and contribution to others.

KEYTAKEAWAYS FROM CHAPTER FOUR

Greatness Within:
Chapter 4 focuses on recognizing and unlocking the greatness within ourselves, emphasizing that everyone possesses inherent greatness.

Overcoming Past:
The author shares personal stories of facing setbacks and struggles, highlighting that our past doesn't define us, and it's never too late to start anew.

Resilience and Determination:
The journey of self-discovery and overcoming mistakes is explored, showcasing how resilience and determination can lead to personal growth and fulfillment.

Relationship Challenges:
The author reflects on a secret romance with Brad, facing the dilemma of choosing between the relationship and abandoning herself, leading to deep emotional turmoil.

SELF DEVELOPMENTAL WORKBOOK
PROMPTS

Take some time to identify and write down qualities or strengths you believe reflect your inherent greatness. What makes you unique and valuable?

Empathetic

Optimistic

Kind

Giving

Organized

Creative

Recall a significant turning point in your life where you overcame a setback or challenge. How did it shape your character, and what did you learn from that experience?

_____

_____

_____

_____

_____

_____

_____

_____

Consider a past or current relationship where you had to set boundaries or make a tough decision. Reflect on how it impacted your sense of self and well-being.

_____

_____

_____

_____

_____

_____

_____

_____

_____

Think about a time when you had to make a decision that
required trust in yourself. What was the outcome, and
what did you learn from trusting your instincts?

_____

_____

_____

_____

_____

_____

_____

_____

_____

Write about a time when you achieved a significant external milestone (e.g., landing a job, reaching a financial goal). How did you feel upon achieving it? Did it bring lasting fulfillment or a temporary sense of accomplishment?

_____

_____

_____

_____

_____

_____

_____

_____

PART TWO
UNLEARNING

The Lies That Lead to Doubt, and the Truths
That Wake Up Worthiness

CHAPTER FIVE

DON'T WAIT ON YOUR WEIGHT

Chapter five dives into the damaging lie that many of us have internalized: the belief that our worth is tied to our weight. The author challenges this notion, urging readers to stop waiting on their weight to live fulfilling lives. She asks thought-provoking questions about the costs of buying into this lie, highlighting missed opportunities for joy, connection, and self-expression. Throughout the chapter, she emphasizes the importance of recognizing and challenging limiting beliefs, which often hold us back from embracing life to its fullest. Drawing from personal experiences, the author shares her journey of overcoming body image issues and learning to let go of societal pressures. She encourages readers to replace negative beliefs with empowering truths, emphasizing the importance of self-acceptance and living authentically. This chapter concludes with a powerful message: don't wait on your weight to pursue happiness, fulfillment, and self-love.

KEYTAKEAWAYS FROM CHAPTER FIVE

The Lie of Weight and Worth:

The chapter challenges the damaging belief that our worth is tied to our weight, urging readers to reject this notion and stop waiting on their weight to live fulfilling lives.

Cost of Waiting:

Readers are prompted to reflect on the costs of buying into the lie that they need to wait until they reach a certain weight to fully engage in life, highlighting missed opportunities for joy, connection, and self-expression.

Identifying Limiting Beliefs:

The author emphasizes the importance of recognizing and challenging limiting beliefs that hold us back from embracing life to its fullest, offering tools and strategies

for overcoming these beliefs.

Empowering Truths:

Readers are encouraged to replace negative beliefs with

empowering truths, cultivating self-acceptance and

embracing authenticity in their journey toward self-love

and fulfillment.

SELF DEVELOPMENTAL WORKBOOK
PROMPTS

Reflect on a time when you felt held back by the belief that your worth is tied to your weight. How did this belief impact your actions and decisions?

Consider the costs of waiting on your weight to fully engage in life. What opportunities for joy, connection, and self-expression have you missed out on as a result?

_____

_____

_____

_____

_____

_____

_____

Identify a limiting belief related to your weight or
appearance that you hold. What evidence do you have to
challenge the truth of this belief?

_____

_____

_____

_____

_____

_____

_____

_____

_____

_____

Practice replacing negative beliefs with empowering
truths. Choose one limiting belief to work on replacing
this week, and write down a positive affirmation or
mantra to counter it.

_____

_____

_____

_____

_____

CHAPTER SIX

The Lie: I Should Only Be Seen When I'm Happy

Chapter six challenges the pervasive cultural notion that individuals should only be seen when they are happy. It begins by highlighting the conflicting messages in today's society, where there is a constant stream of both negative news and pressure to maintain a positive facade. This chapter explores the phenomenon of toxic positivity, where individuals feel compelled to suppress or avoid negative emotions in favor of projecting happiness at all times.

The author discusses the detrimental effects of toxic positivity, including the invalidation of genuine human emotions and the reinforcement of a culture of inauthenticity. Many people hide their true feelings out of fear of burdening others or being perceived as weak, leading to feelings of isolation and disconnection.

Practical strategies for fostering genuine connection and emotional authenticity are presented. This includes the importance of conducting a "capacity check" before engaging in deep conversations with others, ensuring that both parties are emotionally available and prepared to offer support. The chapter emphasizes the value of prioritizing authenticity and alignment with one's true feelings in order to cultivate deeper connections and foster a sense of worthiness in oneself and others.

Chapter six challenges the expectation to only be seen when one is happy and advocates for embracing authenticity and vulnerability in order to foster genuine connection and emotional well-being

KEYNOTES FROM CHAPTER SIX

Toxic Positivity:

Explore the concept of toxic positivity, where individuals feel pressured to project constant happiness, and how it can lead to the suppression of genuine emotions.

Cultural Confusion:

Discuss the cultural confusion arising from the simultaneous exposure to negative news and the promotion of "Good Vibes Only," and how this impacts individuals' perceptions of their own emotions.

Capacity Check:

Introduce the concept of a "capacity check" before engaging in deep conversations, emphasizing the importance of emotional availability for both the sharer and the listener.

Authentic Connection:

Highlight the value of authentic connection, even if it means sharing non-positive emotions, and how it can deepen relationships and foster a sense of worthiness.

SELF DEVELOPMENTAL WORKBOOK
PROMPTS

Have you ever felt compelled to hide your true emotions to conform to societal expectations of constant happiness? How did this impact your well-being?

_____

_____

_____

_____

_____

Evaluate your communication style in relationships. Have you ever conducted a "capacity check" before sharing your feelings or experiences? How might this practice improve your connections?

_____

_____

_____

_____

_____

Reflect on a time when you presented a facade of happiness despite feeling differently. How did it affect your sense of worthiness, and what changes could you make to align more with your authentic emotions?

_____

_____

_____

_____

_____

_____

_____

_____

_____

Consider how the cultural confusion between negative news and positive messaging has affected your perception of your own emotions. Are there specific instances that stand out?

_____

_____

_____

_____

_____

CHAPTER SEVEN

The Lie: I Don't Deserve Better

Chapter Seven dives deep into the personal journey of Ella, a remarkable woman grappling with her inner demons and past traumas. Despite her outward success and admiration from others, Ella struggles with a profound sense of unworthiness and self-doubt that stems from her upbringing and childhood experiences.

This chapter paints a vivid picture of Ella's inner turmoil, revealing how she often finds herself in relationships where her love is not reciprocated. Despite her longing for genuine connection and love, Ella's fear of being alone and her deep-seated insecurities lead her to ignore red flags and settle for less than she deserves in romantic partnerships.

The narrative takes a dramatic turn when Ella becomes involved with a man who presents himself as a widower with two daughters. Initially drawn to his charm and apparent stability, Ella overlooks inconsistencies in his stories and red flags in their relationship. However, as their relationship progresses, she begins to unravel the truth: he has been deceiving her about his marital status, and she contracts a sexually transmitted infection (STI) from him.

This pivotal moment becomes a catalyst for Ella's self-realization and growth. Through therapy and introspection, she comes to understand the importance of loving herself first and breaking free from toxic relationship patterns. With the support of her inner circle of friends, Ella finds the strength to end the relationship and reaffirm her worthiness.

This chapter concludes with a sense of empowerment as Ella takes control of her narrative, renaming her ex-partner's contact in her phone to "DO NOT CALL LIAR INFECTION GUY" and assigning a special ringtone to deter any further contact. This act symbolizes her commitment to prioritizing her emotional well-being and refusing to settle for anything less than she deserves.

Chapter Seven is a poignant exploration of self-discovery, empowerment, and the journey towards self-love and acceptance. Through Ella's story, readers are reminded of the importance of valuing oneself and setting boundaries in relationships to cultivate healthy and fulfilling connections.

KEYNOTES FROM CHAPTER SEVEN

Ella's Inner Struggle:

Explore Ella's internal conflict, where despite external success, she battles a deep sense of unworthiness rooted in past traumas.

Relationship Patterns:

Examine Ella's recurrent pattern of entering relationships where her love is unreciprocated, driven by a fear of loneliness and underlying insecurities.

Deceptive Relationship:

Analyze the pivotal relationship where Ella discovers deception about her partner's marital status, leading to a profound realization about toxic patterns.

Self-Realization and Growth:

Follow Ella's journey of self-realization and growth, triggered by the revelation of the partner's deceit and the contraction of an STI.

Empowerment and Boundaries:

Witness Ella's empowerment as she takes control of her narrative, setting clear boundaries by renaming her ex-partner's contact and using a deterrent ringtone.

SELF DEVELOPMENTAL WORKBOOK
PROMPTS

Delve into your own past traumas and explore how they might be influencing your self-perception and relationships.

_____

_____

_____

_____

_____

_____

_____

Recognize recurring patterns in your past relationships. Are there instances where you settled for less than you deserved?

_____

_____

_____

_____

_____

_____

_____

_____

Consider moments in your life where an external event
or realization served as a metaphorical wake-up call,
prompting self-discovery and growth.

_____

_____

_____

_____

_____

_____

_____

_____

_____

Reflect on the importance of setting empowering boundaries in your relationships. What steps can you take to prioritize your emotional well-being?

_____

_____

_____

_____

_____

CHAPTER EIGHT

The Lie: I Don't Have Anything Special to Offer

Chapter Eight delves into the pervasive lie that many people believe: "I don't have anything special to offer." The author passionately refutes this notion, emphasizing that everyone has something unique and valuable to contribute to the world. They argue that authenticity is key; by offering your genuine self, ideas, talents, and gifts, you bring something completely original to the table.

This chapter begins by debunking common excuses people use to justify their inaction, such as thinking that their ideas are not original or that others can do things better. The author asserts that these beliefs are simply untrue and only hold power if one chooses to believe them.

The narrative is punctuated with personal anecdotes, such as the author's experience founding IT Cosmetics and developing innovative products like a powder blush stain inspired by a bag of Cheetos. Despite setbacks and challenges, the author emphasizes the importance of staying true to oneself and persisting in offering unique contributions to the world.

Ultimately, the chapter concludes with a powerful message: each individual possesses an unparalleled essence that no one else can replicate. By embracing one's authenticity and sharing their gifts with the world, they can make a meaningful impact and fulfill their true potential.

KEYTAKEAWAYS FROM CHAPTER EIGHT

Authenticity Over Comparison:

The author Emphasizes the importance of authenticity over comparison, highlighting that genuine self-expression is more valuable than trying to emulate others.

Unique Contributions:

This chapter stresses the idea that everyone has something special to offer and encourages individuals to identify and embrace their unique contributions.

SELF DEVELOPMENTAL WORKBOOK
PROMPTS

List instances where self-doubt hindered your progress. Develop affirmations or strategies to counter negative thoughts and foster self-belief.

_____

_____

_____

_____

_____

_____

Identify three specific areas where you can offer something unique. It could be in your work, relationships, or personal hobbies. How can you amplify these unique contributions?

SELF-IMAGE OPTIMIZATION: JOURNALING
PROMPTS

List situations where effective communication made a significant difference. How can you authentically present your ideas or yourself to resonate better with others?

Consider a situation where effective communication made a significant difference. How can you authentically present your ideas or yourself to resonate better with others?

_____

_____

_____

_____

Recall a time when you faced a setback or failure. What did you learn from that experience, and how did it contribute to your personal or professional growth?

_____

_____

_____

_____

_____

_____

_____

Reflect on personal strengths, talents, and unique qualities. Identify instances where you may have downplayed your abilities due to comparison.

CHAPTER NINE

The Lie: I Need to Please Them in Order to Love Me

In Chapter Nine, Jamie grapples with the pressure to please others, particularly her health-conscious mother-in-law, Vivi, during a holiday gathering. Despite her desire to indulge in a Cinnabon cinnamon roll, Jamie fears Vivi's disapproval and opts for broccoli instead. However, she realizes that seeking approval from others by sacrificing her own desires only leads to disconnection and inauthenticity. Reflecting on her journey toward self-acceptance, Jamie acknowledges the pervasive nature of people-pleasing and its detrimental impact on self-worth and relationships. Through her experience with the cinnamon roll, Jamie learns the importance of embracing her true self and prioritizing her own needs. She encourages readers to cultivate self-awareness, challenge beliefs that drive people-pleasing tendencies, and embrace authenticity to foster genuine connections and live fulfilling lives.

KEYTAKEAWAYS FROM CHAPTER NINE

People-Pleasing Pressure:
Jamie grapples with the pressure to please others,
particularly her health-conscious mother-in-law, Vivi,
during a holiday gathering.

Sacrificing Desires:
Despite her desire to indulge in a Cinnabon cinnamon
roll, Jamie fears Vivi's disapproval and opts for broccoli
instead, sacrificing her own desires to seek approval.

Authenticity and Connection:
Jamie realizes that seeking approval from others by
sacrificing her own desires only leads to disconnection
and inauthenticity.

Self-Reflection:
Reflecting on her journey toward self-acceptance, Jamie
acknowledges the pervasive nature of people-pleasing
and its detrimental impact on self-worth and
relationships.

Embracing Authenticity:
Through her experience with the cinnamon roll, Jamie
learns the importance of embracing her true self and
prioritizing her own needs.

SELF DEVELOPMENTAL WORKBOOK

PROMPTS

Reflect on a time when you felt pressure to please someone else at the expense of your own desires or well-being. How did it make you feel?

_____

_____

_____

_____

_____

Identify any recurring patterns of people-pleasing behavior in your life. What underlying beliefs or fears might be driving these behaviors?

_____

_____

_____

_____

_____

_____

Consider the impact of people-pleasing on your self-worth and relationships. How has it affected your ability to authentically connect with others?

_____

_____

_____

_____

_____

_____

_____

Imagine a scenario where you prioritize your own needs and desires over seeking approval from others. How would it feel? What positive outcomes might result from this shift in mindset?

_____

_____

_____

_____

_____

_____

Brainstorm strategies for embracing authenticity and living in alignment with your true self. How can you begin to honor your own needs and desires while still maintaining healthy relationships with others?

_____

_____

CHAPTER TEN

The Lie: If I Stand Out, I'll Get Kicked Out

In Chapter Ten, the author delves into the societal lie that standing out might lead to rejection, especially focusing on the expectations placed on individuals based on their gender. Through personal stories and observations, the author explores the tendency for women to downplay their success to be liked and the societal pressure on men to tie their worth to professional success. This chapter challenges the notion that women are often liked less when successful, while men are more appreciated. It discusses how these ingrained beliefs from childhood continue into adulthood, causing individuals to hide their true selves and conform to societal norms, ultimately leaving them unfulfilled.

The narrative unfolds with an anecdote about a friend sabotaging her perfect attendance award in school to avoid standing out and being teased. The author emphasizes that these childhood patterns persist into adulthood, affecting how women and men perceive success and react to societal expectations. The discussion touches upon workplace dynamics, where women are judged more harshly for being assertive, and societal norms that limit both genders, pushing them to hide in plain sight.

This chapter encourages readers to recognize when they are hiding their true selves and take steps to break free from these societal norms. It concludes with a powerful message, urging readers to embrace their authenticity, challenge self-limiting beliefs, and recognize that it's never too late to liberate oneself from the fear of being visible.

Chapter Ten provides a thought-provoking exploration of societal expectations, gender norms, and the impact of hiding one's true self, inspiring readers to step into their authenticity

KEYNOTES FROM CHAPTER TEN

Societal Expectations and Gender Norms:

Explore how societal expectations and gender norms
influence individuals to conform and hide their true
selves, particularly focusing on the impact on women's
success and men's worth tied to their professional
achievements.

Childhood Patterns Persisting into Adulthood:
Reflect on how patterns established in childhood
continue to shape behavior and choices in adulthood,
hindering authenticity and fulfillment.

Recognizing Hidden Behaviors:
Encourage readers to recognize moments when they
hide their true selves to fit societal expectations and
consider the impact on their fulfillment.

SELF DEVELOPMENTAL WORKBOOK
PROMPTS

Recall instances from childhood that may have shaped beliefs about standing out and explore how these beliefs manifest in adulthood.

_____

_____

_____

_____

Analyze personal perceptions of success and how they may be influenced by societal norms related to gender.

_____

_____

_____

_____

_____

_____

_____

_____

Reflect on experiences in the workplace and consider instances where conforming to gender expectations affected behavior, decisions, or interactions.

_____

_____

_____

_____

_____

_____

Identify specific actions to break free from societal norms, embracing authenticity, and challenging self-limiting beliefs.

_____

_____

_____

_____

_____

Contemplate strategies for navigating workplace stereotypes, especially for women, and consider ways to promote authenticity without compromising success.

_____

_____

_____

_____

CHAPTER ELEVEN

The Lie: I'm an Imposter and Not Enough on My Own

The author delves into the pervasive belief that \we are not enough on our own, a narrative often perpetuated by fairy tales and societal norms. Through personal anecdotes and reflections, the author explores how this belief manifests as imposter syndrome, where individuals doubt their own abilities and feel unworthy of their successes. This chapter emphasizes the importance of trusting oneself and one's intuition, rather than relying on external validation or the need for someone else to rescue or complete us. By challenging these narratives and embracing our inner strength and resilience, the author argues that we can break free from imposter syndrome and live authentically as the heroes of our own stories. Through examples like Abbey, a single mother who embodies self-confidence and resilience, the author highlights the transformative power of believing in oneself and taking decisive action towards one's goals. Ultimately, the message is one of empowerment and self-discovery, urging readers to recognize their own worth and embrace their innate abilities to navigate life's challenges.

KEY TAKEAWAYS FROM CHAPTER ELEVEN

Imposter Syndrome:

The author explores how societal narratives and fairy tales perpetuate the belief that we are not enough on our own, leading to imposter syndrome.

Trusting Oneself:

This chapter emphasizes the importance of trusting one's intuition and inner strength, rather than seeking external validation or relying on others to rescue or complete us.

Embracing Resilience:

The author highlights the transformative power of resilience and self-confidence, using examples like Abbey, a single mother who embodies self-assurance and determination.

SELF DEVELOPMENTAL WORKBOOK

PROMPTS

Reflect on a time when you experienced imposter
syndrome. What triggered these feelings? How did you
overcome them?

_____

_____

_____

_____

Consider how societal norms and fairy tales have
influenced your perception of self-worth. How can you
challenge these narratives and cultivate a stronger sense
of self-worth?

_____

_____

_____

_____

_____

_____

Explore the importance of authenticity in forming
genuine connections with others. Have you ever
experienced a deep connection with someone who
showed up authentically? How did it impact your
relationship?

_____

_____

_____

_____

_____

_____

Identify a role model or example of resilience, like Abbey, who inspires you. How can you embody similar qualities of self-confidence and determination in your own life?

_____

_____

_____

_____

_____

Develop a plan to break free from imposter syndrome and embrace your inner strength. What steps can you take to trust yourself more and live authentically as the hero of your own story?

_____

_____

_____

CHAPTER TWELVE

The Lie: If I'm Me, I Won't Be Loved

In Chapter twelve, the author celebrates Oprah's birthday with an enthusiastic, off-key song via an audio text.Her friend Paulo questions this bold move, especially considering Oprah's recent Adele interview. Despite the potential awkwardness, she emphasizes the importance of authenticity in your growing friendship with Oprah.

This chapter delves into the fear of not being loved for your true, quirky self.The author discusses the societal pressure to conform and please others, highlighting how inauthentic behaviors often develop in childhood. Authenticity, defined by Merriam-Webster as being "true to one's own personality, spirit, or character," is explored as crucial for genuine connection and love.

The author shares a personal experience at a hiking retreat, emphasizing the gift of being present with others without cell reception. The narrative unfolds, revealing an unexpected friendship with Edward, the editor-in-chief of British Vogue, formed without the influence of societal expectations. This story reinforces the theme of genuine connections formed when individuals show up as their authentic selves.

The chapter concludes with a reflection on revealing the real you, questioning if people know you for what you do or who you are. It emphasizes that stifling human connection by presenting a curated version of oneself can lead to loneliness. The importance of showing up as the true, unedited self for genuine, deep connections is emphasized, making it a daily practice and a lifelong quest for you.

KEYTAKEAWAYS FROM CHAPTER TWELVE

Authenticity Over Conformity:
Emphasize the importance of embracing one's true, quirky self over conforming to societal expectations.

Childhood Influences:
Explore how inauthentic behaviors often develop in childhood, driven by the need for acceptance and belonging.

Definition of Authenticity:

Define authenticity as being true to one's personality, spirit, and character, highlighting its significance in fostering genuine connections.

Unexpected Friendships:
Share personal anecdotes about unexpected friendships formed when individuals show up as their authentic selves, free from societal pressures.

Loneliness and Disconnection:
Highlight the consequences of presenting a curated version of oneself, leading to feelings of loneliness and disconnection in an increasingly tech-driven society.

SELF DEVELOPMENTAL WORKBOOK
PROMPTS

Reflect on a time when you felt pressure to conform to
societal expectations. How did this impact your sense of
authenticity and connection with others?

_____

_____

_____

_____

_____

Consider your childhood experiences and how they may
have influenced your tendency to hide parts of yourself
to gain acceptance. How can you work towards
embracing your authentic self despite these past
influences?

_____

_____

_____

_____

_____

_____

_____

Reflect on moments when you've felt disconnected or lonely despite being surrounded by others. How might presenting your authentic self contribute to a deeper sense of connection and belonging?

_____

_____

_____

_____

_____

Define what authenticity means to you personally. How do you strive to embody authenticity in your daily life and relationships?

_____

_____

_____

_____

_____

_____

_____

CHAPTER THIRTEEN

The Lie: Labels Are Permanent

Chapter thirteen delves deep into the power of labels and how they shape our identities and self-worth. It begins by highlighting how labels, whether given by others or ourselves, can significantly impact our lives, from childhood teasing to online ratings. This chapter emphasizes how easily we internalize these labels, allowing them to become ingrained beliefs about ourselves.

Using the analogy of the reticular activating system (RAS) in our brains, the chapter explains how we selectively focus on information that reinforces our beliefs, whether positive or negative. It illustrates how empowering labels, like those bestowed upon the author's friend Ed by his teacher, can shape one's life trajectory positively.

The narrative contrasts empowering labels with disempowering ones, showing how the latter can hinder personal growth and happiness. The author shares personal experiences and encourages readers to reflect on the labels they've internalized and their impact on various aspects of life.

An exercise is provided to help readers identify disempowering labels they carry, evaluate their effects, and replace them with empowering beliefs. Practical tips are offered, such as intercepting negative thoughts and reinforcing new labels through daily affirmations and visual reminders.

Ultimately, the chapter emphasizes the importance of taking ownership of our identities by consciously choosing the labels we embrace, rejecting those that don't serve us, and rewriting our stories to reflect our true worth and potential. It concludes with the empowering message that we are the authors of our own identities and have the power to change our lives by changing our beliefs and labels.

KEYTAKAWAYS FROM CHAPTER THIRTEEN

Power of Labels:

Labels, whether given by others or ourselves,
significantly impact our identities and self-worth.

RAS and Belief Reinforcement:

The reticular activating system (RAS) in our brains
reinforces our beliefs by selectively focusing on
information that aligns with them.

Empowering vs. Disempowering Labels:

Differentiate between labels that uplift and those that
hinder personal growth and happiness.

SELF DEVELOPMENTAL WORKBOOK
PROMPTS

Reflect on a memorable label from your past that has influenced your self-perception. How has it shaped your beliefs about yourself?

_____

_____

_____

_____

_____

_____

_____

Identify three disempowering labels you currently carry. What impact have they had on your relationships, career, and overall well-being?

_____

_____

_____

_____

_____

Evaluate the role of the reticular activating system in reinforcing your beliefs. How does it contribute to the amplification of certain labels in your life?

_____

_____

_____

_____

_____

_____

_____

Imagine a scenario where you receive an empowering
label from someone you respect. How does it affect your
confidence and sense of self-worth?

_____

_____

_____

_____

_____

_____

PART THREE
TRANSFORMING

The Journey of You:Building Unshakable Self-Worth and Unconditional Self-Love

CHAPTER FOURTEEN

The Secret to Fulfillment: Self-Worth is the Multiplier

Chapter fourteen delves into the concept of true fulfillment and introduces the idea that self-worth is the key multiplier in achieving it. The chapter begins by posing questions about whether readers feel truly fulfilled in their lives, even amidst accomplishments and success. It acknowledges the common sentiment of feeling like something is missing, despite outward achievements.

The author discusses the importance of self-worth alongside self-confidence, growth, and contribution in attaining ultimate fulfillment. Growth is highlighted as essential for personal development, while contribution emphasizes the significance of giving back to others. The chapter stresses that while self-confidence, growth, and contribution are crucial, self-worth acts as the multiplier for true fulfillment.

The author presents a simplified equation for fulfillment, emphasizing the role of self-worth in multiplying the effects of self-confidence, growth, and contribution. Through examples, readers are guided to assess their current fulfillment levels based on these components.

This chapter concludes with the assertion that without a strong sense of self-worth, achieving external success or fulfillment in various areas of life may still leave individuals feeling empty. It emphasizes the importance of internal worthiness in experiencing true fulfillment, regardless of external achievements. The author encourages readers to believe in their inherent worthiness, allowing them to enjoy achievements without feeling unfulfilled and to pursue their goals passionately while maintaining a sense of fulfillment

KEYTAKEAWAYS FROM CHAPTER FOURTEEN

True fulfillment in life goes beyond external achievements and success; it requires a strong sense of self-worth.

Self-worth acts as a multiplier for self-confidence, growth, and contribution, enhancing overall fulfillment.

Growth and contribution are essential components of fulfillment, alongside self-confidence and self-worth.

Without a solid foundation of self-worth, external accomplishments may still leave individuals feeling empty.

Believing in one's inherent worthiness allows for the enjoyment of achievements and a sense of fulfillment regardless of external circumstances.

SELF DEVELOPMENTAL WORKBOOK

PROMPTS

Reflect on a recent accomplishment or success in your life. How did it make you feel? Did it bring a sense of fulfillment? Why or why not?

_____

_____

_____

_____

_____

Assess your current level of self-confidence, growth, and contribution in your life on a scale of 1 to 10. How do these areas contribute to your overall sense of fulfillment?

_____

_____

_____

_____

_____

_____

_____

_____

Evaluate your level of self-worth. Do you believe in your
inherent worthiness, or do you struggle with feelings of
inadequacy? How does this impact your ability to feel
fulfilled?

_____

_____

_____

_____

_____

_____

_____

_____

Consider moments in your life when you felt truly
fulfilled. What were the contributing factors? How did
your sense of self-worth play a role?

_____

_____

_____

_____

_____

_____

_____

Set goals for cultivating self-worth in your life. What actions can you take to strengthen your belief in your own inherent worthiness?

_____

_____

_____

_____

_____

_____

_____

CHAPTER FIFTEEN

Do You See You?

Chapter fifteen takes readers on a journey of self-connection and worthiness through a gripping personal narrative. It kicks off with a vivid account of the author's experience during a hotel fire in London, using it as a metaphor to explore how many people live their lives in a metaphorical survival mode. This survival mode, characterized by disconnection from one's true self, is examined for its detrimental effects – from lacking authenticity to a constant need for external validation.

The narrative dives into the idea that this disconnection is a form of trauma, impacting mental and physical health. Modern technology and social media are identified as contributors to this disconnection, replacing genuine human connection with superficial interactions.

The spotlight turns on the reader, prompting them to consider if they truly see and connect with themselves. The importance of self-love and acceptance is emphasized as crucial elements for building self-worth and leading a fulfilling life.

This chapter provides five powerful shortcuts to boost self-worth, including focusing on positive intentions, practicing compassionate self-talk, and cultivating gratitude. These shortcuts are presented as practical tools to foster self-connection and enhance one's sense of worthiness. Overall, The chapter weaves personal anecdotes, insightful reflections, and actionable strategies into a compelling exploration of the significance of self-connection and worthiness.

KEYTAKEAWAYS FORM CHAPTER FIFTEEN

Survival Mode vs. Authentic Living:
Explore the concept of living in survival mode versus living authentically, and identify areas in your life where you might be disconnected from your true self.

Impact of Disconnection:
Reflect on the detrimental effects of disconnection from oneself, including feelings of loneliness, lack of authenticity, and constant need for validation.

Self-Connection as Healing:
Understand self-connection as a form of healing from
trauma, both mental and physical, and consider how you
can cultivate deeper connection with yourself.

Technology and Social Media:
Examine the role of modern technology and social
media in exacerbating disconnection, and brainstorm
strategies for fostering genuine human connection in a
digital world.

Practices for Self-Worth:
Explore practical strategies for boosting self-worth, such
as focusing on positive intentions, practicing
compassionate self-talk, and cultivating gratitude in
daily life.

SELF DEVELOPMENTAL WORKBOOK
PROMPTS

Think about a recent situation where you felt disconnected from your true self. What were the circumstances? How did you react, and how did it make you feel?

_____

_____

_____

_____

_____

Identify areas of your life where you might be operating in survival mode. Are there patterns or behaviors that indicate disconnection from your authentic self?

_____

_____

_____

_____

_____

_____

_____

Reflect on the impact of disconnection on your mental
and physical well-being. How does it manifest in your
life, and what consequences does it have?

_____

_____

_____

_____

_____

Brainstorm practical ways to reconnect with yourself and foster genuine human connection in your daily life. Consider activities or practices that align with your values and interests.

_____

_____

_____

_____

_____

_____

_____

CHAPTER SIXTEEN

Know Your Why, Then Fly,Girl,Fly

Chapter sixteen dives deep into the importance of knowing your why as a catalyst for pursuing your dreams and goals with unwavering determination. The chapter opens with a poignant personal anecdote from the author's entrepreneurial journey, recounting a pivotal rejection that nearly derailed her pursuit of launching her company, IT Cosmetics. Despite facing numerous setbacks and doubts from others, the author found solace and motivation in her profound why, which fueled her resilience and commitment to her vision.

The author reflects on the universal experience of feeling compelled to pursue something despite facing opposition or skepticism from others. She acknowledges the temptation to give up in the face of adversity but emphasizes the transformative power of knowing one's why as a source of strength and purpose.

The concept of identifying one's why is explored in detail, with the author highlighting its role in providing meaning and direction to one's goals and aspirations. Whether the goal is tangible or qualitative, attaching a deep, personal why to it increases the likelihood of success and fulfillment.

Practical strategies for uncovering one's why are presented, encouraging readers to reflect on their deepest motivations and desires. Examples are provided to illustrate how knowing one's why can serve as a guiding light during challenging times and inspire perseverance in the pursuit of one's dreams.

The chapter concludes with a call to action for readers to identify their own why for believing in their worthiness and pursuing their goals. Emphasizing the importance of revisiting and evolving one's why over time, the author underscores its value as a powerful tool for navigating setbacks and staying committed to the journey forward.

Chapter sixteen urges readers to know their why and embrace it as a driving force for pursuing their dreams and achieving their fullest potential. Through personal anecdotes and practical insights, the author empowers readers to harness the power of their why to overcome obstacles and soar to new heights in their lives.

KEYNOTES FROM CHAPTER SIXTEENTH

The Power of Knowing Your Why:

Chapter sixteen underscores the transformative impact of understanding and embracing your deep, personal why in pursuing goals and dreams.

Resilience Amid Rejection:
The author shares a personal experience of facing rejection, highlighting the importance of resilience and leaning on one's why during challenging times.

Attachment of Meaning to Goals:
Attaching meaning and emotion to your goals through a clear why significantly enhances the likelihood of success and connection with your aspirations.

Goal-Setting on Steroid:
The combination of knowing how to achieve a goal with a profound why creates a potent formula for achieving dreams, described as "goal-setting on steroids."

SELF DEVELOPMENTAL WORKBOOK
PROMPTS

Share a personal or professional setback you've
experienced and explore how knowing your why could
have positively influenced your response.

_____

_____

_____

_____

_____

Rewrite one of your goals as if it has already happened,
infusing it with the belief that it's already true. Then, list
your specific and meaningful why next to the goal.

_____

_____

_____

Reflect on how your why may have evolved over time.
Consider life experiences, shifts in priorities, or personal
growth that might have influenced changes in your
profound why.

_____

_____

_____

_____

_____

Create a daily reminder incorporating the phrase "Know Your Why, Then Fly, Girl, Fly." Use this as a mantra to reinforce the importance of staying connected to your why.

_____

_____

_____

_____

_____

_____

_____

CHAPTER SEVENTEEN

Circle or Cage

Chapter seventeen delves into the intricacies of relationships, prompting readers to ponder whether their social circles empower or disempower them. It stresses the significance of surrounding oneself with supportive individuals who foster authenticity and acceptance. The chapter urges readers to evaluate their current inner circles, considering whether these relationships align with their personal growth and aspirations.

Navigating familial and social dynamics in today's divisive landscape poses challenges, but the narrative advocates for engaging with differing perspectives without judgment or exclusion. Setting healthy boundaries is emphasized as crucial, despite the difficulty, especially for those inclined towards people-pleasing. The analogy of "candle-blower-outers" underscores the importance of surrounding oneself with those who celebrate rather than diminish one's light.

Furthermore, the concept of chosen family is explored, highlighting the idea that our closest relationships may not necessarily be those we were born into, but rather those who support and celebrate our growth. The metaphor of elephants forming a protective circle illustrates the role of an inner circle in supporting and safeguarding individuals during moments of vulnerability or triumph.

Ultimately, the chapter encourages readers to assess whether their relationships create a circle or a cage, prompting them to embrace their worthiness and courage to live authentically. It advocates for curating empowering circles that nurture self-worth and celebrate individual uniqueness, even if it means stepping out of comfort zones.

KEYTAKEAWAYS FROM CHAPTER SEVENTEEN

Evaluate Your Inner Circle:

Reflect on the people around you and assess whether they empower or disempower you. Consider how these

relationships make you feel and whether they encourage
authenticity and acceptance.

Prioritize Supportive Relationships:
Emphasize the importance of surrounding yourself with
supportive individuals who uplift and validate rather
than confine or judge.

Assess Alignment with Growth:
Evaluate your current inner circles and determine
whether they align with your personal growth and
aspirations.

Navigate Diverse Perspectives:
Acknowledge the challenges of navigating familial and
social dynamics, especially in today's divisive
environment. Value diversity of thought and engage with
differing perspectives without judgment.

Set Healthy Boundaries:
Recognize the significance of setting healthy
boundaries, even if it's challenging. Protect your inner

flame from being extinguished by surrounding yourself with those who celebrate your light.

Chosen Family:

Explore the concept of chosen family, understanding that your closest relationships may not necessarily be those you were born into but those who support and celebrate your growth.

Circle or Cage:

Reflect on whether the people you surround yourself with create a circle that nurtures growth or a cage that constrains. Embrace your worthiness and have the courage to curate empowering circles that celebrate your uniqueness.

SELF DEVELOPMENTAL WORKBOOK
PROMPTS

List the people in your inner circle and reflect on how each relationship makes you feel. Consider whether these relationships empower or disempower you.

_____

_____

_____

_____

_____

_____

_____

Identify the traits of individuals who uplift and support you. What qualities do you value in a supportive relationship?

_____

_____

_____

_____

_____

_____

Assess whether your current inner circles align with your personal growth and aspirations. Are there relationships that may need adjustment or reevaluation?

_____

_____

_____

_____

_____

_____

_____

_____

_____

Consider areas in your life where setting healthy
boundaries is crucial. What steps can you take to protect
your inner flame and well-being?

_____

_____

_____

_____

_____

_____

Envision your inner circle as a protective space. How does this visualization impact your understanding of the role your inner circle plays in your life?

_____

_____

_____

_____

_____

_____

_____

CHAPTER EIGHTEEN

Overexposed and Underdeveloped

Chapter eighteen delves into the concept of being overexposed and underdeveloped, drawing on personal anecdotes and observations to illustrate the importance of balancing exposure with personal development. The chapter begins with a recount of the author's encounter with a famous rapper who praised her infomercial, highlighting the idea that success leaves clues and often requires continuous development and hard work.

The narrative discusses the culture of instant gratification and the glorification of popularity without substance, particularly in the age of social media. It warns against relying solely on exposure and popularity without investing in genuine expertise and development. The author shares insights from her experience in journalism and entrepreneurship, emphasizing the significance of maintaining integrity, expertise, and quality in one's endeavors.

Furthermore, the chapter explores the pitfalls of prioritizing short-term gains over long-term sustainability, both in business and personal relationships. It stresses the importance of being a steward of one's own momentum, making intentional choices to align exposure with development. The author shares personal struggles and lessons learned in navigating the temptation to pursue immediate success at the expense of long-term growth and stability.

Readers are encouraged to prioritize personal development and integrity, acknowledging that sustained success requires ongoing growth and alignment between outward exposure and inner development. It offers practical advice for evaluating areas of improvement, committing to growth, and maintaining self-confidence and worthiness amidst the pressures of modern culture.

KEYTAKEAWAYS FROM CHAPTER EIGHTEEN

Balancing Exposure and Development:

Success requires continuous development and hard work alongside exposure. It's essential to avoid relying solely on popularity or instant gratification without investing in genuine expertise and growth.

Integrity and Expertise:
Maintaining integrity, expertise, and quality in one's endeavors is crucial for long-term success and sustainability, whether in business or personal relationships.

Prioritizing Long-Term Sustainability:
Avoid the temptation to prioritize short-term gains over long-term sustainability. Being a steward of one's own momentum means making intentional choices to align exposure with development.

Navigating Temptations:
Acknowledge and navigate the temptations of immediate success, recognizing that sustained success requires ongoing growth and alignment between outward exposure and inner development.

SELF DEVELOPMENTAL WORKBOOK
PROMPTS

Reflect on times when you may have prioritized short-term gains over long-term sustainability in your personal or professional life. What were the outcomes, and what lessons did you learn from those experiences?

_____

_____

_____

_____

Identify areas of personal or professional growth that you want to focus on. Create a development plan outlining specific actions, milestones, and timelines for achieving your goals.

_____

_____

_____

_____

_____

_____

_____

_____

Evaluate your current endeavors or relationships for integrity and expertise. Are there areas where you could improve quality or authenticity? How can you align your actions with your values and principles?

_____

_____

_____

_____

_____

_____

_____

_____

Explore strategies for resisting the temptation of
immediate success and staying committed to your long-
term goals. How can you maintain focus and discipline
in the face of external pressures or distractions?

_____

_____

_____

_____

_____

_____

Assess the alignment between your outward exposure (e.g., social media presence, public image) and your inner development (e.g., skills, values, mindset). Are there areas where you need to realign your actions or priorities to better reflect your personal growth journey?

_____

_____

_____

_____

_____

_____

CHAPTER NINETEEN

Transformations

In Chapter nineteen,the author delves into the often-overlooked aspects of personal growth and change. Drawing parallels between the metamorphosis of a butterfly and our own transformative journeys, the narrative highlights the vulnerable stages one goes through. From the caterpillar liquefying inside the cocoon to emerging with wet wings, the author emphasizes the challenges, self-doubt, and external pressures faced during transformation. Real-life stories, like Lia's journey from homelessness to entrepreneurship and Frederick's transformation from a life of crime to the CEO of Pigeonly, illustrate the resilience and fulfillment that can come from embracing one's worthiness.

This chapter encourages readers to understand that their past or circumstances don't determine their destiny and to embrace the stages of transformation, believing in their innate worthiness to spread their wings and fly.

KEYTAKEAWAYS FROM CHAPTER NINETEEN

Embrace the Journey:
Transformation isn't just about the end result; it's about the process of growth, resilience, and embracing vulnerability along the way.

Believe in Your Worthiness:
Despite the challenges and doubts that may arise during transformation, remember that you are inherently worthy of spreading your wings and reaching your full potential.

Real-Life Inspiration:
Drawing inspiration from real-life stories like Lia's and Frederick's, recognize that transformation is possible for anyone, regardless of their past or circumstances.

Embracing Vulnerability:
Understand that vulnerability is a natural part of the transformation process, and it's okay to feel uncertain or exposed during these stages.

SELF DEVELOPMENTAL WORKBOOK
PROMPTS

Reflect on a time when you experienced a significant transformation or growth in your life. What challenges did you face during this process, and how did you overcome them?

_____

_____

_____

_____

_____

Explore real-life examples of individuals who have undergone transformation, such as Lia and Frederick. What aspects of their stories resonate with you, and what lessons can you learn from their experiences?

_____

_____

_____

_____

_____

_____

Consider any limiting beliefs or doubts you may have about your worthiness or ability to transform. How can you challenge these beliefs and cultivate a sense of self-worth?

_____

_____

_____

_____

_____

_____

Identify any areas of your life where you feel stuck or resistant to change. What steps can you take to embrace vulnerability and lean into the transformation process?

_____

_____

_____

_____

_____

Imagine your life after undergoing a successful transformation. What does fulfillment and success look like for you, and what actions can you take to move closer to this vision?

_____

_____

_____

_____

PART FOUR
KNOWING

You Are Worthy: It's in You, It Is You

CHAPTER TWENTY

Your Ticket to the Moon

"Your Ticket to the Moon," shares a powerful narrative about embracing uncertainty and taking leaps of faith in pursuit of our dreams. The chapter begins with the author expressing their fear of making a significant professional decision without total clarity. However, a conversation with a friend, Jason, changes their perspective when he gifts them a piece of foil from the Apollo 11 mission. This gift symbolizes the idea that sometimes, we need to take a leap of faith even when we don't have all the answers.

The author reflects on the tendency to wait for perfect clarity before taking action and emphasizes that perfectionism can often lead to procrastination and missed opportunities. Instead, they advocate for taking a step forward in faith, trusting that the next right move will reveal itself along the way. Drawing parallels to JFK's bold vision to land a man on the moon, the author encourages readers to embrace uncertainty and pursue their dreams with courage and determination.

Throughout the chapter, the author shares personal anecdotes and insights about the importance of taking action, even in the face of doubt and fear. They highlight the role of faith and belief in manifesting our desires, emphasizing that both self-doubt and self-belief require equal amounts of energy. Ultimately, the chapter serves as a reminder that we are capable of achieving remarkable things when we trust ourselves and take courageous steps towards our goals, one brave move at a time.

KEYNOTES FROM CHAPTER TWENTY

Embrace uncertainty:

The chapter emphasizes the importance of embracing uncertainty and taking leaps of faith, even when we don't have all the answers.

Take action:
Rather than waiting for perfect clarity, take action towards your goals with courage and determination.
Trust the process:

Trust that the next right move will reveal itself along the
way, and have faith in your ability to overcome
challenges.

Shift your mindset:
Choose to focus your energy on hope, faith, and belief
rather than self-doubt and fear.

Believe in yourself:
Recognize your potential for greatness and trust that you
are capable of achieving remarkable things.

SELF DEVELOPMENTAL WORKBOOK

PROMPTS

Reflect on a time when you hesitated to take action due to fear or uncertainty. What held you back, and what was the outcome of your hesitation?

_____

_____

_____

_____

_____

Think about a goal or dream that you've been hesitant to pursue because of uncertainty or self-doubt. What steps can you take to move forward despite your fears?

_____

_____

_____

_____

147

Imagine yourself taking a leap of faith towards your goals. What does it feel like? What do you see yourself accomplishing as a result?

_____

_____

_____

_____

_____

_____

_____

Identify one action step you can take today to move closer to your goals, even if you don't have all the answers. How can you cultivate a mindset of courage and determination as you take this step?

_____

_____

_____

_____

_____

_____

_____

CHAPTER TWENTY-ONE

Who Are You Really Doubting?

In this Chapter, Lisa shares a bold and powerful lesson on worthiness, emphasizing the impact of one's beliefs in a higher power. She encourages readers to examine their faith and its connection to their sense of worthiness. Lisa recounts her personal journey, highlighting her relationship with God and the transformative power of faith. The chapter explores the paradox of simultaneously believing in divine strength and struggling with self-doubt. Lisa challenges readers to distinguish between self-doubt and God-doubt, urging them to trust their Creator over limiting thoughts. She emphasizes that external achievements and societal idols only boost self-confidence, not true self-worth. Lisa introduces a powerful tool: questioning oneself in moments of doubt, asking, "Who am I really doubting? Me or God?" She shares how aligning with her Creator's word became an instant shortcut to worthiness, enabling her to face challenges and embrace her authenticity. The chapter closes with a call to trust in a higher power and a reminder of the unconditional love God has for everyone, regardless of their journey or identity.

KEYTAKEAWAYS FROM CHAPTER TWENTY-ONE

The Power of Faith:

Explores the connection between faith and worthiness, emphasizing the impact of one's beliefs in a higher power on self-perception.

Distinguishing Self-Doubt from God-Doubt:

Encourages participants to reflect on moments of doubt and discern whether they stem from self-limiting thoughts or a lack of trust in their Creator.

Trusting Divine Guidance:

Discusses the importance of trusting in divine guidance over societal expectations and external achievements, highlighting the role of faith in navigating life's challenges.

Embracing Authenticity:

Urges individuals to embrace their authentic selves by aligning with their Creator's word, emphasizing that true worthiness comes from within.

SELF DEVELOPMENTAL WORKBOOK
PROMPTS

Reflect on a time when your faith or beliefs in a higher power influenced your sense of worthiness. How did this experience shape your self-perception?

_____

_____

_____

_____

Identify moments of doubt or insecurity in your life. Consider whether these doubts stem from self-limiting thoughts or a lack of trust in your Creator's plan for you.

_____

_____

_____

_____

_____

_____

Practice discerning between your own thoughts and
divine guidance. Describe a recent situation where you
felt guided by faith or intuition. How did trusting in
divine guidance impact your decisions?

_____

_____

_____

_____

_____

_____

_____

Write a letter to yourself from the perspective of your Creator, expressing unconditional love and acceptance. Reflect on how embracing this love can empower you to cultivate a deeper sense of worthiness and belonging.

CHAPTER TWENTY-TWO

Solos

Chapter Twenty-Two "Solos," delves into the idea that in life, there are no mistakes, only solos. The chapter begins with the author reflecting on her husband Paulo's lack of rhythm despite being Brazilian, a culture known for its musicality and dance. Despite Paulo's struggle to dance, the author persistently teaches him for their wedding dance, which leads to amusing and heartwarming moments.

The narrative then shifts to a dance class experience where the author learns a valuable life lesson. In the midst of struggling to master a dance routine, a classmate becomes visibly upset after making repeated mistakes. The instructor's response, "There are no mistakes in dance class, only solos," shifts the class's energy and perspective. This phrase resonates with the author, leading to a deeper realization about embracing individuality and creativity in life.

This chapter emphasizes the beauty and power of embracing one's unique path and expression, likening it to a solo dance performance. It highlights the importance of celebrating individuality, creativity, and authenticity rather than conforming to societal expectations. The author encourages readers to embrace their "solos" in life and fully commit to their dreams with confidence, joy, and freedom. Ultimately, the chapter inspires readers to become the best dancers of their lives by embracing their individuality and dancing to the rhythm of their own souls.

KEYNOTES FROM CHAPTER TWENTY-TWO

Embrace Individuality:

Life is a dance, and there are no mistakes—only solos. Celebrate your unique rhythm and expression rather than conforming to societal expectations.

Learn from Challenges:

The chapter highlights the author's journey in teaching her husband to dance and draws parallels with life's challenges. Mistakes are opportunities for growth and learning.

Shift in Perspective:

The pivotal lesson from a dance class, "There are no mistakes in dance class, only solos," emphasizes the power of perspective. Shift your mindset from seeing mistakes as failures to viewing them as opportunities for individual expression.

Creativity and Authenticity:

Solos in life are where creativity sparks, ideas are born, and authenticity thrives. Embrace your unique expression and let it shine in every aspect of your life.

Full Commitment:

The best dancer is not the most technically trained but the one who fully commits. Apply this principle to life—commit wholeheartedly to your dreams, goals, and the beauty of your own journey.

SELF DEVELOPMENTAL WORKBOOK
PROMPTS

Recall a moment in your life when you faced challenges or felt out of sync. How did you perceive those moments? Were there valuable lessons or opportunities for growth?

_____

_____

_____

_____

_____

Share an experience where you perceived a mistake but later realized it was a solo—an opportunity for personal expression or growth. How did this shift in perspective impact your mindset?

_____

_____

_____

_____

_____

_____

_____

Consider a dream or goal you've been hesitant to pursue.
How can you apply the principle of full commitment,
dancing to the rhythm of your soul, to make progress?

_____

_____

_____

_____

_____

Identify your unique rhythm in life. What sets you apart? How can you celebrate and express your individuality in various aspects of your life?

_____

_____

_____

_____

_____

_____

_____

_____

CHAPTER TWENTY-THREE

You Are Worthy-Your Victory Lap Starts Now

The author reflects on the profound impact her mother, Nina, had on her life, starting from the day of her adoption to Nina's final moments. She shares how Nina's love and support shaped her upbringing, especially during challenging times with her adoptive father's struggles with addiction and infidelity. Despite the hardships, Nina's unwavering love and resilience taught Jamie valuable lessons about strength, perseverance, and the importance of staying true to oneself.

As Jamie recounts her mother's battle with illness in her later years, she describes the emotional toll of watching Nina's health decline and the role reversal that occurred as she became the primary caregiver. Jamie's devotion to her mother during this time highlights the depth of their bond and the profound impact Nina had on Jamie's life.

The chapter delves into a pivotal moment during Nina's final days, where she imparts a powerful lesson to Jamie: the importance of recognizing one's inherent worthiness. Nina's words, "Don't change," serve as a catalyst for Jamie's realization that true fulfillment comes from embracing one's authentic self, rather than striving for external validation or success.

Jamie shares her journey of self-discovery and acceptance, acknowledging the weight of unworthiness that she carried throughout her life and the liberation she experienced upon embracing her inherent worthiness. She encourages readers to embark on their own "victory lap" of self-acceptance and empowerment, promising to support them every step of the way.

Chapter twenty-three serves as a poignant tribute to Jamie's mother and a powerful reminder of the importance of self-love and acceptance in achieving true fulfillment in life.

KEYTAKEAWAYS FROM CHAPTER TWENTY-

THREE

Maternal Influence:

Explore the significant role of maternal figures in shaping one's identity, emphasizing the impact of love, resilience, and life lessons passed down from a mother like Nina.

Resilience and Strength:

Highlight the theme of resilience in the face of adversity, as portrayed through Jamie's recollections of her mother's ability to endure challenges and maintain strength throughout life.

Role Reversal:

Examine the emotional complexities of role reversal in caregiving, especially in the context of watching a parent's health decline. Reflect on the transformative nature of such experiences.

Authenticity and Self-Discovery:

Delve into Jamie's journey of self-discovery, triggered by her mother's poignant advice of "Don't change." Explore the concept of embracing one's authentic self and the impact on overall well-being.

Inherent Worthiness:

Discuss the revelation of inherent worthiness as a central theme. Explore the idea that true fulfillment comes from recognizing and accepting one's worth, independent of external achievements or validation.

SELF DEVELOPMENTAL WORKBOOK
PROMPTS

Recall significant moments or lessons from maternal figures in your life. How have these influenced your values, perspectives, or resilience in the face of challenges?

_____

_____

_____

_____

_____

_____

Share a personal story of resilience during challenging times. How did you navigate adversity, and what lessons did you learn from those experiences?

_____

_____

_____

_____

_____

_____

_____

_____

Consider a time when you felt pressure to conform or change for external validation. How did it affect your well-being, and what did you learn from that experience?

Reflect on your own sense of worthiness. How much does it depend on external factors, and how might recognizing your inherent worth impact your overall happiness and fulfillment?

_____

_____

_____

_____

_____

_____

_____

_____

WORTHY DOESN'T END HERE

In the closing words of "Worthy," Jamie Kern Lima extends an invitation to continue the journey together as victory lap partners for life.

Additionally, Lima introduces the concept of the Victory Lap Card, inspired by library cards. Readers are encouraged to pass the book on to others, whether by gifting a copy or physically passing it along. The Victory Lap Card allows individuals to document and celebrate each person who receives the book, creating a ripple effect of empowerment. Lima emphasizes the potential to positively impact the world, one person at a time, by spreading the message of worthiness.

As a final note, she suggests that readers can pass the baton to themselves, acknowledging the value of revisiting the book and discovering new insights as personal growth unfolds. The message resonates with the idea that each reading can offer a different experience based on one's evolving perspective and journey.

ABOUT PAVILION READS

Are you constantly overwhelmed by never-ending to-do lists, looming deadlines, and a packed schedule that leaves you with no time to indulge in the books you've been longing to read? Look no further! PAVILION READS is here to revolutionize your reading experience and cater to the needs of busy individuals just like you.

At PAVILION READS, Our mission is simple: to offer detail-oriented, straight-to-the-point, and exceptional quality workbooks and summaries of life-changing books authored by the world's most renowned writers. Imagine immersing yourself in the remarkable ideas and insights of thought leaders, self-help gurus, and groundbreaking intellectuals, all while efficiently managing your busy schedule.

Our commitment to excellence is unwavering. Each workbook and summary produced by PAVILION READS is carefully crafted, ensuring a seamless reading experience that captures the essence of the original book. We understand that your time is precious, which is why we guarantee that every page you read from our workbooks will be valuable, enlightening, and life-enhancing. Whether you're seeking personal growth, professional development, or simply a moment of respite from your hectic life, PAVILION READS is your trusted companion.

Join the PAVILION READS community today and unlock a world of knowledge and inspiration, tailored to fit the needs of your busy lifestyle. With our comprehensive workbooks and summaries, you can make every minute count, and embark on a journey of

Made in United States
Orlando, FL
18 July 2024